D1399980

A GUY'S GUIDE

Who Are These People?

Coping with
Family Dynamics

ABDO
Publishing Company

A GUY'S GUIDE

Who Are These People?

Coping with
Family Dynamics

by Michael Fallon

Content Consultant
Dr. Robyn J. A. Silverman
Child/Teen Development Expert and Success Coach
Powerful Words Character Development

Credits

Published by ABDO Publishing Company, 8000 West 78th Street, Edina, Minnesota 55439. Copyright © 2011 by Abdo Consulting Group, Inc. International copyrights reserved in all countries. No part of this book may be reproduced in any form without written permission from the publisher. The Essential Library™ is a trademark and logo of ABDO Publishing Company.

Printed in the United States of America,
North Mankato, Minnesota
062010
092010

 THIS BOOK CONTAINS AT LEAST 10% RECYCLED MATERIALS.

Editor: Mari Kesselring
Copy Editor: Richard Reece
Interior Design and Production: Marie Tupy
Cover Design: Marie Tupy

Library of Congress Cataloging-in-Publication Data
Fallon, Michael, 1966-
  Who are these people? : coping with family dynamics / Michael Fallon.
    p. cm. — (Essential health : a guy's guide)
  ISBN 978-1-61613-545-4
  1. Boys—Family relationships—Juvenile literature. 2. Boys—Psychology—Juvenile literature. 3. Families—Juvenile literature. 4. Communication in families—Juvenile literature. 5. Interpersonal relations—Juvenile literature. I. Title.
  HQ775.F35 2011
  646.7'8083—dc22
                                2010017367

contents

Dr. Robyn Silverman truly enjoys spending time with young people. In fact, it's what she does best! As a child and teen development specialist, Dr. Robyn has devoted her career to helping guys just like you become all they can be—and possibly more than they ever imagined. Throughout this series, you'll read her expert advice on friends, girls, classmates, school, family, and everything in between.

A self-esteem and body image expert, Dr. Robyn takes a positive approach to life. She knows how tough it is to be a kid in today's world, and she's prepared with encouragement and guidance to help you become your very best and realize your goals.

Dr. Robyn helps young people share their wildest dreams and biggest problems. Her compassion, openness, and honesty make her trusted by many adolescents, and she considers it a gift to be able to interact with the young people whom she sees as the leaders of tomorrow. She created the Powerful Words Character Development system, a program taught all over the world in martial arts and other sports programs, to help guys just like you become examples to others in their communities.

As a speaker, success coach, and award-winning author, Dr. Robyn's powerful messages have reached thousands of people. Her expert advice has been featured in *Prevention* magazine, *Parenting* magazine, *U.S. News and World Report*, and the *Washington Post*. She was an expert for *The Tyra Show*, *Fox News*, and NBC's *LXtv*. She has an online presence, too. You can follow her on Twitter, become a fan on Facebook, and read her blog on her Web site, www.DrRobynSilverman.com. When she isn't working, Dr. Robyn enjoys spending time with her family in New Jersey.

Dr. Robyn believes that young people are assets to be developed, not problems to be fixed. As she puts it, "Guys are so much more than the way the media paints them. They have so many things to offer. I'm ready to highlight how guys get it right and tips for the ways they can make their teen years the best years so far . . . I'd be grateful if you'd come along for the ride."

Take It from Me

Growing up can be difficult for guys. As you get older, you often face tough decisions about what is right and wrong and how you should act. You have to deal with social pressures from kids your own age, and you feel the weight of your family's expectations. Sometimes you feel crazy energy that you don't know how to control. Other times you may make impulsive decisions and regret them later.

I know from my own experiences that families can either add to or take away from a guy's problems. Some families are supportive, and many of us have caring parents and siblings. Other families can cause a lot of trouble. Still, pretty much everyone has things they like and dislike about their families.

In this book, I'll talk about some of the challenges that guys face in dealing with their families, as well as some of the good things families can provide. We'll look at a wide range of different family situations. In particular, you'll learn how your relationship with your parents can affect your life—how overprotective parents may make you feel trapped and rebellious, while "cool" and permissive parents may cause you trouble. We'll look at how a divorce or a missing father can affect your life and what to do about it. And we'll look at sibling relationships—like what to do when a younger brother or sister constantly pesters you or how to handle sibling rivalry.

Some of these issues have no easy answer or quick fix. But one good first step in dealing with any family issue is to learn what lies at the root of the problem. If you know why you are frustrated with your family, or why they are frustrated with you, you can develop strategies to solve the problems—or at least make life more tolerable.

Learning to deal with family problems will help you gain some important skills. This will make it easier for you to deal with the pressures of growing up and prepare you for your life as an adult.

A Guy Who's Been There,

Michael

1

Respecting Mother

Dear old Mom. At times she can be so caring and connected to you. When you've fallen off your skateboard and banged up your knee, she's the one you go to for first aid. When you've had a really bad day, she's there to comfort you. Other times, though, it seems as if she has no idea what your life is like. She's clueless about what you are going through at school, with friends, and in your social life. Sometimes, she can seem hopelessly out of touch.

If it seems like your mother doesn't understand you, you may be tempted to push her away rather than try to explain your problems to her. When you think she's treating you unfairly, you may even get mad and yell at her. That's not the answer, though. In fact, you may just be harming yourself. Studies show that guys who have good relationships with their mothers are happier as they get older. And guys who get along with their mothers tend to have better and longer-lasting relationships with the other people in their lives.

So, go easy on your mom, even when you're frustrated with her or tired of what seems to be clueless advice. When you learn to respect your mother's judgment and point of view, you learn to respect yourself. Just take it from Aiden.

Aiden's Story

Aiden was a good kid who got pretty decent grades throughout elementary school. In middle school, though, things started to get tough. The friends he had hung out with in elementary school went to a different middle school, and they had all made new friends there. For a while, he'd tried to hang out with his old friends on the weekends, but now it seemed like they were always busy. Aiden felt really nervous when talking to new people, so it was difficult for him to make new friends in his new school.

when you learn to respect your mother's judgment and point of view, you learn to respect yourself.

Aiden was also maturing somewhat early for his age. He was tall and gangly compared to most of his classmates. He also developed bad acne. Some kids teased him. They called him "Stretch" and "Freckles." Aiden hated the way he looked and how the other kids treated him. He felt like a freak. During lunch at school, he often ate alone. Watching the other kids from a distance, he began to think he'd never fit in.

Eventually, Aiden did find a few kids to sit with at lunch. They were kids like him who often got teased for being different. It was nice because these kids didn't make fun of him like everyone else. Aiden and his new friends would sit on the far edge of the cafeteria at lunch and make fun of what conformists the other kids were. Aiden started dressing in black. He even dyed his hair black.

Think About It

- Why does Aiden feel like a "freak"?

- Have you ever felt like an outsider among your peers or classmates? What did you do about it?

- Why do you think Aiden started dressing in black and dyed his hair black?

Aiden was moody at home. He avoided talking to his parents. He especially avoided his mother, who was always telling him to "smile more." She would buy him brightly colored clothes, but Aiden never wore them. They were the same stupid brand-name clothes that all the jocks at his school wore. Every day after school Aiden's mother would say, "How was your day, honey?" But Aiden didn't have anything to tell her. He was annoyed that she was even asking. He felt his life wasn't any of her business and that she didn't understand him at all.

One evening, when Aiden refused to come down for dinner, his mom came into his room.

"Are you okay?" she asked. Aiden didn't even look at her.

"Mind your own business," he said angrily. "Just leave me alone!"

Aiden's mother looked hurt. She shook her head and left the room. Aiden felt so angry. Why was his mom always bothering him? She had no idea what his life was really like.

Think About It

• Why does Aiden avoid talking to his mom?

• How do you think Aiden's mother feels about his behavior?

• Why does Aiden think his mom doesn't understand his problems?

The next day, Aiden's friend Brent tapped him on the shoulder during lunch.

"You free after school today?" Brent asked.

"Yeah, what's up?" Aiden replied.

"You know Hannah Nelson?"

Aiden nodded. Hannah was a really popular girl at school.

"I wanna egg her house," Brent whispered, smiling.

"Really?" Aiden was a little surprised. Neither of them really knew Hannah.

Aiden's mother looked hurt. She shook her head and left the room.

"Yeah, it'll be fun. You've gotta help me," Brent said.

"Yeah, okay," Aiden agreed.

Brent was right. Throwing eggs at Hannah's house was a lot of fun—at least until Hannah's parents called the cops. Aiden and Brent ended up at the police station. Aiden knew his mom was going to freak out.

Aiden's mother picked him up at the police station. In the car on the way home, she finally spoke to him. "Aiden, you're grounded. Indefinitely."

Aiden just shrugged. He figured as much. When they got home, his mother made him sit down with her in the kitchen.

"Aiden," she said, "we have to do something about your behavior. What's wrong? You haven't been yourself for months."

"Myself?" Aiden shot back. "You don't know who I am!"

"I know when you aren't happy, Aiden. I'm your mother."

"You don't know anything about me!" Aiden yelled, getting up from the table. "You want me to be happy? Then just leave me alone!"

Aiden's mother started crying into her hands. Aiden felt terrible. He'd made his own mother cry. But he stormed out of the kitchen.

Think About It

- Why do you think Aiden agreed to help Brent throw eggs at Hannah's house?

- Do you think it was fair of Aiden's mother to ground him?

- Why do you think Aiden's mother started crying? Have you ever made one of your parents or guardians cry? How did you feel about it?

During your preteen and early teen years, your body undergoes very rapid physical, psychological, and hormonal changes. Those changes can be confusing and difficult to manage, and they often make guys your age moody, temperamental, and unpredictable in their emotions and actions. At the same time, becoming more independent from your parents is a normal part of growing up.

Problems happen when a guy's natural urge for independence comes in conflict with his parents' expectations. Many mothers are used to nurturing their children from an early age, something a kid really appreciates when he's younger. But when you start to feel a natural desire for independence, Mom's nurturing can feel like she's smothering you. Lashing out at your mother probably won't help the problem. Conveying your feelings to her in a productive, respectful way is vital to the relationship and to your own sense of character.

It's important to keep in mind that your mother won't stop caring for you and worrying about you—and you for her. And mothers can be pretty great. Even when we're older, they can be our best supporters and sounding boards when we need to talk.

Work It Out

1. Find balance between establishing your own independence and remaining respectful of your parents. Start by accepting that your mother will want to know what is going on in your life.

2. What if it feels like your mom's interest in your life is out of line, like she's prying? Reassure her. Tell her that you respect her right to know about the important parts of your life, but that it is important for you to have some privacy as well.

3. If you get into a fight with your parents, this doesn't mean that you don't respect and love them. The fights are short-lived, but your relationship with your parents lasts. Growing up is difficult. Remember that your growing up can be difficult for your parents, too.

The Last Word from Michael

I know it is not always easy to get along with your mother. Sometimes it can feel like she is simply there to spy on you and keep you from having fun. Other times it feels like she will never understand you. But don't give up on her. Talk with her and strike a deal that shows you respect her right to know what you're going through, even as it allows you some freedom to become who you're meant to be.

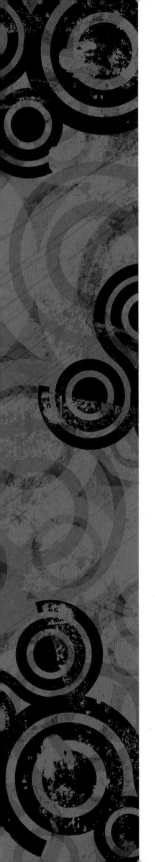

2 Overprotective Parents

o you think your parents still treat you like a little kid? Are they unfair, refusing to let you do fun and exciting things with your friends? Do you feel you'll never get to experience life if they don't lighten up?

If that's how you feel, the good news is you're not alone. Most guys experiment with new things during their adolescence. Sometimes guys push boundaries of "acceptable" behavior. This is part of the natural process of discovering what is right and what is wrong. The bad news is that parents, who have lived longer and experienced more than you, naturally will seek to keep you away from anything they know is harmful. This conflict—between your desire to experiment and experience new things and their desire to protect you—can lead to lots of tension in your family.

But even the most daredevilish guys and the most protective parents eventually survive this period. Like Omar and his overprotective parents.

Omar's Story

By the time he reached seventh grade, Omar had developed a healthy interest in girls. He liked talking to them. They had different interests and viewpoints from his guy friends. Then, in eighth grade, Omar met Molly. She was a year older than he was, but she had just moved to his neighborhood.

One day Omar found out that some high school kids were having a house party and that Molly was planning to go. Omar wanted to be

Sometimes guys push boundaries of "acceptable" behavior. This is part of the natural process of discovering what is right and what is wrong.

there, but he knew what his parents would say: "High school kids are too old for you. You'll have plenty of time later to go to parties."

Omar's parents were stricter than most of his friends' parents. Omar hadn't been allowed to go on a sleepover until he was ten. And even though he was 14 years old now, he still had to get his parents' permission to see a PG-13 movie. Sometimes Omar worried that his parents would turn him into a social outcast.

But Omar *had* to go to the party. He really wanted Molly to see that he could be just as cool as the high school guys she hung out with. So he began plotting a way to attend.

Think About It

• Is it normal for Omar to be interested in Molly? Why or why not?

• Why is Omar interested in the high school kids' party?

• Have you disagreed with a decision your parents made over something you wanted to do? How did you deal with the situation?

Omar and his friend Chris came up with a plan to go to the party. Chris's room was located on the far backside of his house on the ground level, so he could come and go through the window as he pleased without his parents knowing.

Omar asked his parents if he could go see a movie with Chris on Friday night and spend the night at Chris's house afterwards. His parents, after asking a few questions about which movie it was and

what time they would be home, agreed. They knew Chris and his parents well.

The next night, the guys met at Chris's house. Chris told his parents they were going to play video games all night. They turned on some music and locked Chris's door. They waited until Chris's parents had gone to bed. Then they opened up the back window of Chris's room and slipped out. The party was only a few blocks away, and as they started walking there both of them laughed nervously. Omar couldn't wait to see Molly's face when he showed up.

Think About It

- Do you think Omar's decision to lie to his parents about the party was the right thing to do? Why or why not?

- Have you ever lied to your parents? How did you feel? What were the consequences?

- Do you think Omar would attend the party without Chris?

By the time Chris and Omar reached the party, it was already late. Things were in full swing. Omar's first impression was that it was really noisy. There was loud music and lots of people shouting. Most of the kids were drinking beer. A lot of them were smoking, too. He saw a few kids passed out in the backyard. One kid was sick in the bathroom. Omar even saw a few couples making out in front of everyone. Omar suddenly felt like coming here was a huge mistake.

"C'mon!" yelled Chris when Omar lagged behind. "You've got to find Molly!"

Chris didn't seem to mind the chaos. Omar looked around for Molly, but he couldn't find any sign of her. Instead, he nearly got caught in the middle of a fight.

Omar suddenly felt like coming here was a huge mistake.

He managed to duck out of a room just as one guy slammed the other into a wall.

Omar lost track of Chris. It took him a half hour to find his friend in the wild crowd. Chris

was chatting with some high school girls who were drinking beer and smoking cigarettes outside.

"This is crazy!" Omar said. "Let's go."

"No way!" said Chris. "I'm just starting to have fun. You can go home if you want."

"Fine," Omar grumbled.

Omar walked all the way to his own house. When he got home, his parents were surprised. They asked him what had happened. Omar couldn't think of any more lies, so he told them the truth.

"You shouldn't have lied to us," Omar's mom said.

"You're grounded for the next two weeks," said his dad.

Omar frowned. Two weeks was a long time.

"We would've grounded you for a longer time," his father said. "But you did the right thing by leaving the party and telling us the truth now."

Think About It

- Is Chris a good friend to Omar? Why or why not?

- What might have happened if Omar had stayed at the party?

- Have you ever confessed to lying about something? What happened when you told the truth?

Your parents will always love you no matter what, but trust is a separate issue from love. Trust doesn't naturally occur in every relationship. It has to be earned over time. Every action you take and every word you say affects the level of trust between you and your parents. You have to work to build your parents' trust. Your parents have to know that, even though you may make some mistakes, you will always try to do the right thing.

A solid step toward building your parents' trust in you is to first acknowledge that they often know what's best for you. After all, they love you, and they have lived longer and experienced more than you. Their insights into what's right and what's wrong have some merit.

What if your parents are especially protective, even after you feel you've proven yourself to be responsible and trustworthy? That can be tough. Try to remember that your parents only want you to stay safe. Do your best to understand and follow their rules.

Work It Out

1. Trust starts with communication. This means talking to your parents and letting them know about your life.

2. You will often discover you have different ideas from your parents. But try to understand their views on an issue and respect their opinion. They are, after all, in charge of things—at least until you move out on your own.

3. With some parents, the best thing you can do is try to strike a compromise. For example, if your parents won't let you go to a party where there'll be high school kids, ask your parents if you can have a party at your house that they can monitor, instead. That way you'll still get to invite that cute girl you want to get to know.

The Last Word from Michael

Impatient as you are to grow up, there's no need to hurry. You'll have plenty of time to do things you're not allowed to do now. For the time being, relax and enjoy yourself. Be thankful your parents are concerned, and try to be glad that they're watching over you. Soon enough, you'll have more responsibilities than you ever bargained for—including, perhaps someday, a child of your own to worry over.

3

Cool Mom

Not all parents are overprotective. Some aren't protective enough. These are called permissive parents. Often, permissive parents give their child almost everything he wants to avoid any conflict. As their kid moves into his teenage years, these parents may treat him more like a buddy than a child. They may try to win his affection with gifts and money. Such parents may even be reluctant to discipline their children when they have done something wrong.

Do parents like this sound like a dream come true? If you actually have permissive parents, you probably don't think so. You might feel like they don't care about you because they make no

effort to keep you out of dangerous situations. While your friends' parents want them home for dinner by 6:00, you might stay out until midnight without so much as a sharp word from your mom or dad. Find out how Ty felt about his "cool mom."

Ty's Story

Ty's mom was considered the "cool mom" by all of Ty's friends. Though she worked long hours as a nurse, she made it up to her son by buying him a smart phone and lots of other high-tech gadgets. She also let Ty go wherever he wanted on weekday nights. On weekends, she would drive Ty and his friends all around the city.

Often, permissive parents give their child almost everything he wants to avoid any conflict.

Often, Ty's mom took Ty and his friends to the mall and let them wander around by themselves until it was time for her to pick them up. Sometimes she took them to concerts and amusement parks. She let Ty go to parties without asking who was going to be there. And she let Ty go downtown by himself.

Think About It

- why do Ty's friends think Ty's mom is a "cool mom"?

- Do you wish your mom were more like Ty's mom? why or why not?

Sometimes Ty felt like his mother didn't really care about him because she never asked where he was going or where he had been when he got home. Sometimes he wondered if she would even notice if he never came home at all.

One day at school, Ty started talking to some kids he had seen smoking cigarettes outside the mall on weekends. After school, he met up with them behind the school building. They offered him a cigarette, and he tried smoking it. It burned his nose and he coughed a lot, but Ty felt like these kids accepted him more than his other friends. He started hanging out with them a lot.

Soon, Ty's mom was driving him and his new friends to the mall on weekends. But they would usually sneak out back to smoke cigarettes and hang out. And they invented a game where they would throw rocks at the cars in the parking lot. Then they would run away from mall security.

One day when Ty came home from school, his mother was in the kitchen holding the pack of cigarettes he'd been hiding in his sock drawer. Ty sucked in his breath and prepared himself for the lecture of his life. But instead, his mother tossed the pack of cigarettes at him. He caught it.

"Don't let me find these again," she said, and started to walk out of the room.

Ty sucked in his breath and prepared himself for the lecture of his life.

"Aren't you going to yell at me?" Ty asked, looking at the crumpled cigarette carton in his hand.

"You're a good kid." Ty's mom shrugged. "I don't want to fight with you. Everyone experiments with stuff like that at your age. You'll outgrow it."

Think About It

- why do you think Ty began smoking?

- How do you feel about smoking?

- why do you think Ty's mom doesn't worry about Ty's smoking? Do you think she should have done something about this? why or why not?

A few months later, one of Ty's friends gave him a bag of marijuana for a birthday present. Ty didn't really want to try it. He had noticed that his teeth were turning yellow from the cigarettes. It was kind of gross. He wondered what smoking marijuana could do to him. But Ty stashed the marijuana in his room in case he changed his mind.

A few days later, Ty discovered that the marijuana was gone. He wasn't surprised. He was sure his mother had taken it. He hadn't tried very hard to hide it. For a while, Ty expected his mother to talk with him about the marijuana. He was going to explain to her how his friends had gotten him into some things that were wrong for him, and he was

planning to quit. But when she never said anything, Ty felt confused and disappointed. Didn't she care about him at all?

Think About It

- What do you think Ty wants from his mother?

- How would you feel if your parents caught you doing something wrong and they never said anything to you about it?

Parents who act like best friends to their kids are doing them a great disservice. Such parents fail to provide guidance. As a guy grows up, he is learning how to become a responsible adult. He needs the modeling, structure, and insight that he gets from his parents. Ty was frustrated because his mother did not provide the guidance that he needed.

If your parents are permissive, you might feel alone. You might even believe that no one cares what happens to you. If so, it's probably time to sit down with your parents and let them know how you feel. If you want things to change in your family, you might need to be the person to take a stand.

If talking with your parents doesn't work, seek out guidance from another adult. The parents that we are born to are not always the best role models. Luckily, role models can easily be found. Next time you're wondering whether you should be doing a certain behavior, don't think about what your permissive parents would say. Instead, how would your favorite coach, big brother, or grandmother feel about your actions?

Work It Out

1. Talk to your parents about how you are feeling. They might not realize how their permissiveness affects you.

2. Set some rules for yourself. What kind of a person do you want to be? What do you want to achieve in your life? Make a list of your goals. Make another list of ways you can achieve these goals. Then, make a third list of things that might keep you from reaching your goals, such as drugs, dropping out of school, or being arrested.

3. Find another adult you can talk to. If your parents aren't able to provide you with good advice and rules, talk to another family member, coach, teacher, or friend.

The Last Word from Michael

Permissive parents crave your acceptance, but they still love and care about you. Having permissive parents is both good and bad. On the upside, you probably learn how to take care of yourself and how to handle new situations sooner than a lot of guys your age. The bad side is that without examples and guidance, you might get into trouble that could seriously affect your future. And even if you avoid trouble, you could become an adult who is still looking for a clear sense of right and wrong.

4

Divorced Parents

Most kids cannot imagine their parents splitting up. However, studies have shown that nearly half of all American marriages since 1970 have ended in divorce. That means that a lot of guys have to deal with divorced parents. If your parents break up, you might be frustrated and have a hard time understanding this change in your life. You might be angry with one or both of your parents. But if your parents fought a lot when they were married, you might feel relieved when they are no longer living together.

Miguel's parents divorced when he was 11. He was confused by the changes this caused in his life, and he tried hard to understand what was happening to his family.

Miguel's Story

Growing up, Miguel was a pretty happy guy. He didn't have any brothers or sisters, but he had a lot of friends. He liked sports and was a starter on his hockey team. Miguel tried to study hard and always do his homework. When he came across a problem he didn't understand, he went to both his mother and father for help. His father helped him with math, while his mother seemed to know the definition of every difficult word.

As Miguel got older, he noticed that his parents seemed unhappy with each other. They fought a lot and sometimes slept in separate bedrooms. When Miguel was in sixth grade, his parents sat him down and told him that his dad was moving out—they were getting a divorce.

Miguel felt tears forming in his eyes. He couldn't believe what was happening.

If your parents break up, you might be frustrated and have a hard time understanding this change in your life.

"Your father and I still love you very much, Miguel," his mother assured him.

"I promise I won't miss a single hockey game," said his father. "And if you need help on your math homework, all you have to do is call."

Think About It

- Why does Miguel start crying when he learns his parents are getting a divorce?

- How do you think the news of his parents' divorce affected Miguel?

- Why does Miguel's father promise that he'll never miss Miguel's hockey games?

Miguel's parents shared custody of Miguel after the divorce. During the week, Miguel lived with his mother in the house where he had grown up. Money was tighter now, so Miguel's mother worked a second job. Sometimes she didn't come home until late.

Miguel saw his father, who had moved to an apartment across town, on weekends. Despite his father's promise to never miss a hockey game, Miguel noticed that his father missed many games.

"Why don't you come to my games anymore?" Miguel asked his father one weekend.

"I'm sorry," Miguel's father said. "I've got to work. But I make it to most games, don't I?"

Miguel thought about his hockey teammates. Their dads were always in the stands cheering them on or shouting out tips. Miguel's father used to be one of those fathers. Now, half of the time, no one was there to see Miguel play.

"You're a liar!" Miguel said suddenly. "You promised to come to all my games." Miguel rushed to his bedroom, his eyes stinging with hot tears.

Think About It

- Why do you think Miguel is upset with his father? Is it just about the hockey games?

- Have your parents ever disappointed you? How did you react?

Frustrated with his life at home, Miguel began to care less about school. He failed several tests, but neither his mother nor father noticed. Soon, Miguel was failing in both math and English. When his report card arrived at his mom's house, she made Miguel take it with him over the weekend to show to his dad. Miguel planned to hide the report card in his bag and never tell his dad about it. But his dad was already expecting to see it.

"Can I see your report card?" he asked the moment Miguel walked in the door.

Reluctantly, Miguel dug out the report card from the bottom of his backpack and handed it to his dad. Miguel's dad squinted at the bad grades, as if he couldn't believe he was seeing them.

After a minute or two of uncomfortable silence, Miguel's dad spoke.

"Well, I think you'll have to quit the hockey team until you can get your grades up," he said.

"What?" Miguel yelled in outrage.

Think About It

- why do you think Miguel starts to do worse in school after his parents' divorce?

- why is Miguel angry when his father tells him he has to quit the hockey team?

- Do you think Miguel's father is being fair? why or why not?

That Monday, Miguel stopped by his hockey coach's office after school.

"Hey, Coach Burns," he said.

"What's up, Miguel?" Coach asked.

"I've got some bad news," Miguel said, sitting down in a chair. "My dad says I've gotta quit the team to get my grades up."

Coach Burns looked confused. "That is bad news," he said. "I thought you were a good student? What happened?"

Miguel felt his face burn red. He looked down in his lap. Before he knew what was happening, tears were running down his face. "I don't know. . . . Ever since my parents got divorced. . . ." he managed to choke out. When Miguel finally looked up again, Coach Burns was frowning deeply.

Before he knew what was happening, tears were running down his face.

"I know what you're going through," Coach Burns said. "My parents got divorced when I was about your age."

Miguel nodded, wiping away his tears. It felt good to know that Coach Burns understood how he was feeling.

"I'll tell you what, Miguel. I'd really like to keep you on the team. I'm gonna give your dad a call. I bet we can get you some extra help so you can stay on the team and improve your grades."

Miguel smiled for the first time in a long time. "Thanks, Coach," he said, getting up to leave.

"No problem," said Coach Burns. "I know it isn't easy to talk about this stuff, but my door is always open."

Think About It

- why does Coach Burns take an interest in Miguel's problems?

- Do you know a teacher or other adult who is helpful like Coach Burns?

- Do you think Miguel will be able to stay on the hockey team? why or why not?

Divorce can be disruptive to your life in many ways that you might not expect. As parents deal with the problems related to divorce—such as poor finances, complicated scheduling, and other life problems—they might have less time to devote to you than they did in the past. So after a divorce, you might feel like you are getting less attention from your parents. Miguel missed the attention he used to get from his parents when they were together.

Some parents might be uncomfortable talking about the divorce with you. But talking about your feelings after a divorce can be really helpful. It is not a good idea to keep your feelings bottled up inside. If your parents aren't interested in talking, find another family member, coach, teacher, or even a friend whom you can talk to and who will listen to you.

Work It Out

1. If you are worried and confused about your parents' divorce, don't keep your feelings bottled up. Start by asking your parents about the divorce and how life will be after everything is finalized.

2. If your parents resist talking to you, or if you don't get the answers you need, try talking about your feelings to someone else, such as a grandparent, an older sibling, or a favorite aunt or uncle.

3. Remember that your parents' divorce is not your fault. You are still an important part of their lives. They love you.

4. Remember that you are not alone. Many families go through divorce every year. There are a lot of kids your age dealing with divorces right now.

The Last Word from Michael

Going through the divorce of your parents can be very difficult. The life you knew is suddenly disrupted. You feel confused and even guilty about what role you might have played in your parents' breakup, even though the reason has nothing to do with you. Your family feels pretty strange for a while. But they are still there for you. It is just different than it was before.

5

Perfect Sister

o you have older siblings? Do you get along with them? You might have had a rivalry with a sibling for almost as long as you can remember. According to some psychologists, sibling rivalry is particularly intense when children are very close in age and of the same gender. A rivalry can also be very intense when one child gets better grades than other children in the family.

Sibling rivalries are normal. But they can also be frustrating. If you have an older sibling who seems to excel at everything, you might feel pressured to be just as successful. People might constantly compare you to your older sibling. This can be difficult because, although your sibling and you grew up in the same family, you probably both have very different interests, personalities, and skills. While your sibling might be an incredible athlete, you might be more skilled at music. Read on to find out how Danny dealt with his rivalry with his big sister.

Danny's Story

Danny entered middle school the year after his sister, Emily, graduated from the same school. Emily was a top student in her class and a favorite of all her teachers. Emily seemed to excel in every subject. She was good at math, science, social sciences, and English. She took first place in the district spelling bee competition. She even played clarinet in the school orchestra. For most of his life, Danny had felt like he stood in his sister's shadow.

In his classes that fall, Danny was surprised to learn that many of his teachers had very high expectations for

> For most of his life, Danny had felt like he stood in his sister's shadow.

him. On the first day of math class, his teacher, Mr. Adams, smiled at him as he came into the classroom. Danny had never even met Mr. Adams, but he'd heard his sister talk about him. Once Mr. Adams had gone through the plan for the course, he pointed to Danny.

"This young man," Mr. Adams said as Danny shrunk in his chair, "is the younger brother of one of the best students I've ever had. If Danny is anything like his sister, this class is going to have a tough time keeping up!"

Danny felt his face turn bright red. He could hear some of his friends giggling in the back. Danny was terrible at math.

Think About It

- Why do you think Danny's math teacher, Mr. Adams, singles out Danny on the first day of class?

- Is it fair for Danny's teachers to have such high expectations for him when he starts middle school? Why or why not?

- Have you ever been singled out because of something your sibling did? How did you feel about it?

Danny quickly discovered that all of his teachers expected him to be as good a student as Emily. He could tell they were disappointed when they handed back his papers or tests. His grades were pretty good. They just weren't the straight As that Emily always got. Danny's English teacher, Ms. Lewis, even took

him aside after class and said, "You should ask your sister for some help with your essay. She's a very good writer."

Danny just nodded. He could see no reason to try in school if everyone expected him to be just like his sister. No matter what he did, he would be a disappointment. He wasn't Emily.

That day, Danny came home to find Emily reading a book on the porch.

"Danny," Emily said, not even looking up from her book. "All your baseball stuff is in the hallway. Can you pick it up? I keep tripping on it."

"Stop bugging me," Danny muttered.

Emily still didn't look up. "I'm just asking! You know I like things clean."

Angrily, Danny snatched the book out of her hands and threw it across the backyard.

"Why do you have to be so perfect?" he yelled.

"Geez, Danny!" Emily complained as she went to retrieve her book. "What's your problem?"

Think AbOut It

- Has anyone ever expected you to be just like your brother or sister? How did it make you feel?

- Why did Danny throw Emily's book and yell at her? Do you think it was fair of him to do that?

- Do you think Emily understands why Danny is frustrated with her?

During second trimester, Danny started taking art with Mrs. Williams. While he had always liked drawing and painting in his spare time, he had never thought of taking a real art class before. He had

picked art simply because he didn't want to take the other option—band. He knew the music teacher would just compare him to Emily, who was great at the clarinet.

Danny had fun on the first few assignments. They were mostly drawing, and Danny had been

sketching pictures since he was pretty young. One day, Mrs. Williams asked the class to draw a self-portrait for homework.

That night, Danny worked really hard on the assignment. He set up a mirror next to his desk so he could easily look at himself while drawing. Danny stayed up really late working on the portrait. Emily walked past his bedroom on her way to bed. "Wow," she said. "You're really working hard on that drawing." Danny just smiled and kept working.

A few days after Danny turned in his self-portrait, he was walking into art class when he saw his drawing hanging on the display board outside the classroom. He was surprised.

Danny stayed up really late working on the portrait.

"Hey," Danny said as he entered the classroom, "Mrs. Williams, why is my self-portrait hanging up out there?"

Mrs. Williams just smiled. "Because it's one of the best works of art I've ever seen from a student at this school."

Think About It

- Have you ever taken a class on a subject that was completely new to you?

- Why do you think Danny has so much fun doing his art assignments?

- Why is Danny surprised when Mrs. Williams hangs his self-portrait on the display wall?

Although siblings often share certain family characteristics, each child in a family is an independent person. Each person has his or her own special talents, interests, and personality traits. Your brother's or sister's abilities in certain areas really have little to do with you. You will develop your own abilities and skills as you grow up.

While it is natural for people to compare siblings and for siblings to compare themselves to each other, always keep in mind that it doesn't matter how you measure up. In fact, comparing yourself to a sibling can hold back your own development. It can also cause frustration and tension in your relationship with your sibling.

Instead of comparing yourself to others, you are better off developing your own skills, strengths, interests, and talents. When you focus on what makes you unique, you will discover that other people recognize those special qualities in you.

Work It Out

1. A good rule for life—not just for dealing with your siblings—is to stop comparing yourself to others.

2. Focus on discovering things about yourself. Don't be afraid to experiment. Try all sorts of things.

3. Once you've learned what makes you happy—whether it's art or tap dancing, ice fishing or water polo—pursue these things regardless of how your siblings choose to spend their time.

The Last Word from Michael

I know from experience how easy it is to compare yourself to others. I have done that often while trying to decide how well I was doing in school, in my job, and in my life. And other adults I know also spend a lot of time comparing themselves to others and worrying about it. They look at how big a house their friends have, how nice their cars are, how well-behaved their children are, and so on. In the end, though, none of this comparing makes anyone happier. So my advice is this: always avoid comparing yourself to others. Instead, try to be happy for others' accomplishments and keep reaching for your own.

6

Annoying Little Bro

Ah, younger siblings. They're so easily impressed, and they follow you around as if they worship you. They can be cute and fun to be around, with all their questions and wide-eyed interest in everything you're doing. And let's face it, when you discover them imitating you, it's flattering. But, at the same time, sometimes you wish they'd just leave you alone. When you're tired after a long day of school and practice and everything else, the last thing you want is a younger brother bugging you. It's especially hard when he follows you around, comes into your room, and asks a bunch of stupid questions. Often, it seems as if your younger brother was put on Earth just to bother you at the worst possible times.

But having a younger brother also gives you the opportunity to set a good example for someone younger than you. You can be a person he looks up to and comes to for advice about sports or girls. Find out how Matthew learned the responsibilities of being a big brother.

Matthew's Story

Matthew was a busy guy. He participated in lots of after-school activities. He spent long hours taking pictures for the school paper, practicing with the school's band, playing on the basketball team, and working on student council. Matthew enjoyed these activities; they made him feel important.

> Often, it seems as if your younger brother was put on Earth just to bother you at the worst possible times.

Matthew's brother, Ethan, was six years younger than he was. Ethan seemed to love everything that Matthew did—the same music, movies, and sports teams. Ethan even pretended that a paper towel tube was a trumpet, because Matthew played trumpet in his school's band. When Matthew's baseball hat got too ratty for him to wear any more, Ethan begged to have it. Matthew gave it to him, and Ethan had been wearing it ever since.

Because of all of Matthew's after-school activities, he got home each day several hours later than Ethan. So, Ethan was almost always waiting for him with a ton of questions.

"What did you do today?"

"How was practice?"

"Did you take that big math test?"

"What are you doing tonight?"

It seemed like the questions went on and on.

Think About It

- Why does Ethan take so much interest in Matthew's likes and activities?

- Are you involved in a lot of school activities? Why or why not?

- Do you have a younger sibling? Do you get along with him or her?

Matthew was usually flattered that his brother was so interested in his life. More than once, though, Matthew had to tell Ethan to leave him alone so he could finish his homework or whatever else he might be working on. Matthew started to find it irritating that Ethan was always pestering him with questions and following his every move. It also annoyed him

that Ethan thought he could like everything that Matthew liked. Why couldn't Ethan find his own interests?

One day, Matthew had a huge pile of homework when Ethan came marching into his room as usual.

"Hey, Matt!" said Ethan. "Do ya know what a velociraptor is?" It was Ethan's new game to ask Matthew about all the different dinosaurs he was learning about in school. Matthew often played along, but not tonight.

Matthew groaned. He looked at the large pile of homework on his desk. "I don't know."

"Guess! Come on!"

If Ethan didn't stop bugging him, Matthew would never get all his work done. "I don't know!"

Matthew yelled. "Don't you have little kid friends to play with?"

Ethan looked up at Matthew from under the brim of the large baseball hat. Big tears welled up in Ethan's eyes, and he dashed out of the room.

Matthew slammed his bedroom door shut. He tried to focus on his studying, but he felt bad about Ethan.

Think About It
- why was Matthew flattered when Ethan first started paying attention to him?
- Have you ever made a sibling cry? How did you feel about it?
- Are your siblings allowed to come in your room? why or why not?

A few minutes later, Matthew's dad came into his room.

"What's going on with you and Ethan?" his dad asked.

"I didn't do anything! I'm trying to study, and he was bothering me," Matthew explained. "He asks me like a hundred questions, and he won't go away!"

Matthew's dad smiled a little. "Well, you're his big brother. He looks up to you."

Big tears welled up in Ethan's eyes, and he dashed out of the room.

"I guess," said Matthew. "But it's so annoying."

"I'll talk to him and let him know that he can't bother you when you're doing homework," his dad

promised. As Matthew's dad turned to leave the room, he paused for a minute. "By the way, Ethan told me yesterday that you're the coolest big brother in the whole world. Not bad, huh?"

Matthew shrugged and turned back to his homework. But he had to admit, it was nice to know that Ethan liked him so much. Matthew decided that after he was done with his homework, he'd take Ethan down to the park. Maybe Ethan was old enough to learn the rules of basketball.

Think About It

- why does Matthew's dad tell him what Ethan said about him?

- why does Matthew decide to take Ethan to the park?

- Do you think you are a role model for anyone? In what ways do you think you are or could be a role model?

It is very normal for siblings in a family to annoy one another. When people spend a lot of time together, the tension of dealing with everyday life can lead to short tempers, raised voices, and misunderstandings. Often, because of the stress in your life, a sibling who is just trying to be nice or who shows interest in your life may become a perfect target for your frustrations. You may snap at your younger brother without even knowing why you are upset.

Though losing your temper at a younger sibling may be natural, it probably won't help the problem or make you feel any better about it. And, while you may want to just ignore your little sibling, this won't make him or her disappear. Instead, try speaking calmly to your sibling and explain the situation. Strike a balance between time with your sibling and time for yourself. After all, your sibling loves you and looks up to you, so you want to be a positive and considerate role model.

Work It Out

1. If you need some space from your sibling, explain in a kind tone that you are tired or have work to do.

2. If you get tired of answering endless questions, or you simply want some privacy, put a limit on the number of questions your sibling can ask you.

3. Get help from your parents. They might be able to entertain your sibling when you need some space.

4. Remember that being a big brother is a big responsibility. Your younger sibling will copy a lot of what you do, so it's important to set a good example.

The Last Word from Michael

One of the hardest things to do when you're busy growing up is to think about the future. This is particularly true when you're frustrated with an annoying younger sibling who doesn't seem to get that you have your own life. Keep in mind, though, that you and your sibling have long lives to live. If you lash out at your younger sibling today, you may end up affecting your relationship for many years to come. At the moment, your younger sibling is taking an interest in you because he looks up to you. But this interest probably won't last. Eventually, your sibling will become more independent. So, for now, try to enjoy, but not abuse, the attention.

7

The Worker

D o you sometimes look at your friends at school—at their great clothes and the cool stuff they have—and wonder if everyone but you is rich? Do you listen to your father worrying about how he's going to pay the bills each month? Have you ever had to skip a meal because the money had run out before your mother's next paycheck? If so, you're far from alone. According to recent studies, about 39 percent of the nation's children—nearly 29 million in 2005—live in families officially designated as low income.

Family economic hardship can be a day-to-day struggle. In some families, guys might be called upon to start working to help the family keep up with the bills. Working to assist your family can be both challenging and rewarding. You have less time to focus on your homework and friends, but you receive work experience that will help you in the future, and you can take pride in being a source of income for your family. Take Logan, for example. He had to get a job to help his family.

Logan's Story

working to assist your family can be both challenging and rewarding.

Logan was the oldest kid in his family of six. For most of his life, he felt like a normal kid. Money was always tight in his family, but both his parents worked hard so that everyone was taken care of. Then one summer Logan's world was turned upside down. His father was hurt in a bad car accident. He had worked in a warehouse, but because of his injuries, he would be out of work for several months. Logan's mother's salary as a secretary became the family's only source of income.

One night, a few days before school started that fall, Logan's father took him aside after dinner.

"Son," Logan's father said, "your mother and I have been talking. We think it'd help out the family if you could contribute some money this year. Mrs. Thompson needs a babysitter four times a week after school. A few of the neighbors could use someone to mow their lawns, too. What do you think?"

Logan felt a lump growing in his throat. He was disappointed. He wanted to play soccer this school year. And, he was planning to start a band with his friends. With these jobs, he would have no time for either.

Think About It

- Do you think it is fair for Logan's parents to ask him to work to help support the family?

- Do you think Logan is selfish for being disappointed about his own plans when his family has money problems?

- What would you do if your family suddenly needed you to work to help support them?

"What do you say, Logan?" his father asked. "Can you help us out?"

Logan looked into his father's eyes. They looked so sad and pleading. He knew how upset his father had been since the accident. Things hadn't been the same since. If this was a way he could help things get better, he had to do it.

"No problem, Dad," he said.

Logan worked things out with Mrs. Thompson. He babysat her son every weekday after school except Thursday. He also mowed lawns on Saturday, but he

had Sunday off to catch up on homework and other things.

Working was more difficult than Logan thought it would be. It was hard for him to keep up with his schoolwork, and he was tired at school. His friends kept calling him to hang out, but it seemed like Logan always had to work.

One day, Logan came home from school to eat something quickly and head off to his babysitting

job. His brother Tommy was in the front yard, bouncing a soccer ball from knee to knee.

"Hey, Logan!" Tommy exclaimed. "Guess who made the soccer team?"

Logan's heart dropped into his stomach. It was unfair that Tommy got to play soccer while he had to spend all his free time working! Logan just nodded at Tommy and headed into the house.

> Logan's heart dropped into his stomach. It was unfair that Tommy got to play soccer while he had to spend all his free time working!

In the kitchen, he saw his little sister Abby pouring a nearly full bowl of cereal into the trash can.

"Abby!" Logan yelled. "What are you doing?"

Abby looked puzzled. "What?" she said. "I'm done with it."

"You're so stupid!" Logan yelled. He tried to dig the soggy cereal pieces out of the trash. "That stuff costs money! I work really hard so that you and the other kids get to eat!"

"You sound just like Mom!" Abby exclaimed and dumped the rest of the cereal into the trash before running upstairs.

Think About It

- Do you think Logan's jobs are a good thing for him?

- Why do you think Logan is acting more like a parent than a kid?

- Have you ever had a job? What did you do? Did you enjoy it?

Logan looked at his hands covered in cereal bits. Abby was right. He was acting like his mom. Logan kicked the trash can over.

When Logan came home from babysitting that night he was so tired and frustrated with the whole day that he almost crashed on the couch. As he was going upstairs to go to bed, he heard the front door open. His mom was home from work.

"How was babysitting?" she asked. "Want some lemonade?"

"It was fine," Logan said coming into the kitchen with her. Logan saw that there were dark circles under his mom's eyes. She looked exhausted. Yet she was still willing to make lemonade for him. Logan thought about how hard his mother had always worked for her family. Suddenly, he felt guilty that he resented having to work so much.

Logan's mother passed him a cup of lemonade. "I really appreciate all you're doing to help out the family, Logan," she said. "I don't know what I'd do without you."

Think About It

- Why does Logan feel guilty after he notices how tired his mom looks?

- How do you think it made Logan feel to hear that his mother appreciated him working?

- Has a parent ever told you that he or she appreciated work you do?

If your family faces a money crisis and you are able to step in and help the family by working, it can feel good. Even if you only make a little bit of extra money, it can make a difference to your family. Having a job can also teach you good work habits and help you understand the value of money.

But working to help your family is not easy. It can add a lot of pressure to your life. It also limits the choices you can make for yourself. While your friends are playing sports or dating girls, you might be too busy for any of those activities. If working to help your family is too stressful, and your grades and social life suffer as a result, have a chat with your parents. Remember your first responsibility is to keep yourself happy, healthy, and successful, both in school and out.

Work It Out

1. If your family asks you to get a job to help with income, seriously consider it. It can be very rewarding to help out your family.

2. See if you can get a job that relates to your interests. If you like sports, maybe you can get a job coaching a community team.

If you like being outside, mowing lawns or other yard work might be a good fit for you. Just because it's "work" doesn't mean it can't be fun!

3. Remember that you are still a kid who is developing social and other skills. Promise that after you finish your schoolwork and the work at your job, you will set aside a few hours each week for yourself.

4. If working becomes too stressful or time consuming, let your parents know. Even working two days a week could be a big help to your family, while allowing you time for school and other activities.

The Last Word from Michael

Family money problems can be tough on everyone in the family. Your parents will stress over every unpaid bill and every upcoming expense. Their stress, in turn, will affect everyone else in the family. Working a job to help relieve that stress can be really helpful. You can also be proud to know that you did everything you could to help your family, even as you learn valuable lessons about how to be a good and responsible worker. And who knows? At work you may meet new friends and find skills you never knew you had!

8
Fatherless

Many kids in the United States live in fatherless families. In fact, the number of fatherless families has been rising for many years. Growing up without a father can be tough on guys. If your father left your mother before you were born or when you were very young, you might feel responsible for his disappearance, even though it is not your fault. You might feel abandoned or unwanted. If you never met your father, you might wonder where he is and if he has any other family. You might feel left out when your friends are spending time with their fathers. And no matter how much you love and appreciate your mother, a part of you might wish your father was around, too. You might even feel embarrassed that you don't have a father.

But it is important to remember that families come in all shapes and sizes. Try not to let not having a father at home affect how you feel about yourself. Wyatt's father left before he was born. He spent years feeling like an outsider—until he realized that no family is perfect.

Wyatt's Story

Wyatt never knew much about his father. He knew that his mother met his father at a dance club when she was still in high school. And he knew that his father's name was Adam. Wyatt's mother never liked to talk about his father. If Wyatt asked her any questions about him she usually said, "I don't know," or, "He was a jerk. That's all you need to know."

Wyatt also knew his father had left town when he learned that Wyatt's mother was pregnant and that Adam and his mother did not know each other very well. He understood that his mom might not want to talk about Adam, but it was frustrating sometimes. Even if his dad was a jerk, didn't Wyatt deserve to know something about

> It is important to remember that families come in all shapes and sizes. Try not to let not having a father at home affect how you feel about yourself.

his own father? Most of the time, Wyatt didn't mind being raised by just his mother. She had to work a lot, but he usually thought she was a good mom.

Think About It
- Why do you think Wyatt's mother doesn't want to talk about Wyatt's father?
- Do you think Wyatt deserves to know more about his father?

One day in social studies, Mr. Peters announced that the class would be making family trees. Wyatt almost groaned. He only knew one side of his family. He'd had to do a family tree in elementary school once, and it looked stupid and empty on one side. Most of Wyatt's classmates didn't know that his dad wasn't in the picture. And Wyatt didn't really want them to know.

Wyatt watched as Mr. Peters drew his own family tree on the whiteboard. "Put your mother's name on one side and your father's name on the other," Mr. Peters instructed. As Wyatt watched Mr. Peters chart out his perfect family tree on the whiteboard, he felt even worse.

"Spend some time on this tonight," Mr. Peters said. "We'll share our family trees in class tomorrow!"

After class, Wyatt went up to talk to Mr. Peters. "Uh, Mr. Peters?" Wyatt said. "I don't think I can do this assignment."

Mr. Peters raised his eyebrows. "Why not?" he asked.

Wyatt hesitated. "I . . . I don't have a dad, okay? I only know one side of the tree." He gestured towards Mr. Peters's perfect tree on the whiteboard.

"That's okay, Wyatt," Mr. Peters said. "Just do the part you know."

Wyatt frowned. All the kids in the class were going to laugh when they saw that Wyatt knew nothing about his father.

Think About It

- Have you ever had to do a family tree for a class? Did you enjoy the assignment? Why or why not?

- Do you think Mr. Peters is being fair? Why or why not?

The next day, Wyatt walked into social studies with his lopsided family tree. He sunk down at his desk and kept the paper turned over so that no one could see it.

"Everyone have their assignment?" Mr. Peters asked as class started. "Bring your trees up to the front, and we'll tape them on the wall."

Wyatt dragged his feet as he walked up to the wall. He slowly applied tape to the edges of the paper. Then he quickly stuck the paper on the wall and hurried back to his desk. Maybe no one would realize that it was his family tree.

But as Wyatt watched other kids hang up their family trees, he was surprised. Only a few of the trees looked like the one Mr. Peters had done. The others were all different shapes. Some kids only had one parent's history just like Wyatt. Others had information about their birth parents and their adoptive parents on their trees. Some were

missing information on grandparents or even great grandparents. Still others listed stepparents and stepsiblings. Wyatt looked at his own tree in the corner of the wall. It wasn't that different after all.

Think About It

- what did Wyatt learn from seeing his classmates' family trees?

- what does your family tree look like? How many parents do you have? How many siblings?

The most important thing to remember if you live in a fatherless family is that it's not your fault that your father did not stick around. And just because your father isn't around doesn't mean you can't grow up to be a decent man yourself.

Wyatt felt self-conscious because he thought his family was different from his classmates' families. But he learned that all families are different. There is no such thing as one normal type of family.

That said, it might be difficult to grow up without a male influence in your life. If you are looking for a role model, try a coach, a teacher, or a relative. There are also many mentor programs you can join where you will find good, supportive men.

Work It Out

1. Know that, despite the difficulties you face, you are loved by your mother and other family members.

2. If you feel like you need an older male to look up to, see if you have an uncle or a male family friend who might like to hang out with you from time to time.

3. Make a pledge that you will never abandon a child if you become a father someday. You can be part of the solution!

4. Remember that all families (even the ones that look completely normal) are different and unique. There is no such thing as a perfect family.

The Last Word from Michael

Being raised without a father can be tough. If you've never met your father, you may wonder about him all your life. But not having a father doesn't mean that your life isn't important and that you can't make something of yourself! Many people raised in fatherless families have gone on to lead great lives. One example is President Barack Obama. Most important, you have the opportunity to become a good and decent man who will help other people by becoming a positive role model.

9

The Adopted Kid

Adoption is a legal process that allows someone to become the parent of a child, even though the parent and the child are typically not related by blood. People who cannot or do not want to bear children themselves can become parents by adopting children whose birth parents are unable to care for them. Parents who adopt children do so because they want to build a family.

Adopted kids are not born to their parents. Instead, they are chosen. Their parents love and care for them just like other parents. However, if you were adopted, you may sometimes have a little more on your mind than your friends do. As he got older, Dakota thought all the time about the fact that he was adopted.

Dakota's Story

Dakota grew up in a typical family in the suburbs of a large U.S. city. He was no different from any suburban kid who liked to ride skateboards and bikes. When he was in grade school, Dakota's parents told him he was adopted. Dakota was not sure what to think about it. His family was the only family he had known. So, the idea that he had been born to someone else was hard for him to understand.

Adopted kids are not born to their parents. Instead, they are chosen. Their parents love and care for them just like other parents.

Think About It

- why do you think Dakota's parents waited until he was in grade school to tell him he was adopted?

- were you or anyone you know adopted?

Dakota didn't think much more about being adopted until he got older. He found himself wondering more and more about his birth parents. What kind of people were they? Where did they live?

Did they have any other kids? Did they look or act like him? How would his life have been different if they were still his parents? And, most important, why had they put him up for adoption in the first place?

None of Dakota's friends were adopted and most of them didn't know Dakota was adopted. He didn't have anyone to talk to about his questions, and he wasn't really sure he wanted to talk about being adopted anyway.

One day when Dakota came home from school, his mother was frantically cleaning the house.

"Aunt Ellen is coming over for dinner tonight. I need you to pick up your room and take Max for a walk," she said as soon as he walked in the door.

"But, Mom," Dakota said, "I was gonna play football with the guys tonight! I promised!"

"Well, I need your help." She tossed the dog's leash at Dakota. "Walk him now, please."

Dakota stomped out of the house with the dog. It wasn't fair. Dakota wondered if his birth mother was a nicer person than his real mom. Maybe his birth parents missed him and wanted him back. Dakota wondered why his parents had adopted him at all. They didn't get along with him very well these days. They didn't even seem to understand who he was anymore.

For the next few weeks, Dakota thought about his birth parents so much that he started having trouble paying attention in school. Some of his teachers noticed that he wasn't keeping up. One day as he was leaving math class, Ms. O'Brien stopped him.

"Hey, Dakota," she said. "Is everything okay? I've noticed you seem to have a hard time paying attention lately."

Dakota just shrugged. "It's nothing," he said. "I'll try harder in class." He raced out of the classroom before Ms. O'Brien had a chance to ask any more questions. Dakota was too embarrassed to explain that he was thinking about his birth parents. He didn't like the thought of telling anyone that he was adopted.

Maybe his birth parents missed him and wanted him back.

After a couple of months, Dakota's teachers told his parents that he was doing poorly in school. Dakota's parents had always paid attention to his schoolwork, so they immediately sat down with him to have a talk.

"What's wrong, Dakota?" asked his mother. "Is someone at school picking on you?"

"Is the work too difficult?" asked his father. "We could get a tutor if you need one."

Think About It

- why do you think Dakota has so many questions about his birth parents?

- why does Dakota not want to tell anyone he was adopted?

Dakota didn't want to tell his parents the truth. He was afraid it would make them sad and maybe even jealous if they knew he'd been thinking about his birth parents so much. Even though they didn't always get along, Dakota still loved his parents and he didn't want to hurt them.

"If you don't tell us, we can't help," said Dakota's mother.

Finally, Dakota took a deep breath. He knew he had to say something. He was trying to figure out the best way to explain what was going on when he heard himself burst out, "I just don't understand why they didn't want me!" Dakota was surprised when tears started forming in his eyes. "Am I that awful that they didn't want to keep me?"

Think About It

- What do you think Dakota's parents will say next?

- Do you think it is normal for Dakota to feel like he was abandoned?

- Do you think Dakota will be glad he told his parents the truth? Why or why not?

An adopted child's curiosity about his birth parents is natural. Sometimes guys who are adopted are afraid to talk about these feelings. They may feel happy about their homes and their adoptive parents and yet still have a lot of questions or feelings of loss. It is completely natural to feel this way.

If you are adopted and have questions or concerns, don't keep your feelings to yourself. Talk about them, whether you are scared, confused, sad, or angry. Your feelings are normal, and there are lots of people who can help you work through them. Try your parents first. Let them know that you love them, but that you are having trouble with some feelings about being adopted. If you feel like you can't talk to your parents, try talking to another relative or a school counselor. They can help you learn more about your feelings and also open the door to discussion with your parents.

Work It Out

1. Remember that you are no different from anyone else. Yes, not everyone is adopted. And yes, adoption can sometimes be difficult to understand. But you are so much more than just the "adopted kid."

2. Remember that just because you were adopted, it does not mean that your birth parents didn't want you. They may simply have been unable to care for you due to money issues or other factors. They likely wanted to give you the best life possible with a loving family who could afford to give you the life you deserved.

3. Remember that your parents always want you as their son. You may not have been born to them, but in every other way, you are their son and they love you.

4. See if you can find some other adopted kids living in your area. You're not as alone as you think! There may even be some networks that you can find online.

The Last Word from Michael

I have had a number of friends who grew up with adoptive parents. Adoption was often something these friends thought about. But it wasn't the only thing in their lives. That is, while each person was aware that he or she had been adopted, each one was also interesting and gifted in his or her own way. Each friend I've known who was adopted was really just the same as friends I've known who were not adopted. They were individuals, each with their own set of traits, interests, talents, and abilities.

10
The Soldier's Son

Families with one or more parents in the military are all over the United States. These families must deal with the pressure of their loved ones leaving, sometimes to go to dangerous places for months at a time. They often face economic hardships as well. Kids in these families can have a difficult time dealing with the constant change and unpredictability of military life.

Being the son of an active soldier can be really tough. You might worry about the safety of your parent while he or she is deployed. Your parent might miss special events in your life. While you can usually keep in contact through phone calls and e-mails, you may not hear from your parent for long periods of time. Because his dad was in the military, Malik would not see him for several months at a time.

Malik's Story

Malik's father served in the U.S. Army. He was a dedicated soldier. The military needed good soldiers, so Malik's father was deployed for several long tours in Afghanistan, beginning when Malik was very young. Because of this, Malik's father had missed some important moments in Malik's life. He'd missed seeing Malik perform the lead in the school play a year ago. He also had not been home to watch Malik in track for the last two years. None of Malik's friends had parents in the military. Their moms and dads seemed to never miss an event. Malik felt that no one really understood what that was like for him.

Being the son of an active soldier can be really tough. You might worry about the safety of your parent while he or she is deployed.

When Malik's father came back home from deployment, he often seemed different. Sometimes he'd stare out into space or look nervous when they were driving in the car. Malik sometimes felt like he didn't know what to say or how to act around his dad. Lately, Malik was changing so much that it felt like he and his father had to get to know each other

all over again every time his dad came back home. It always took a while for things to get back to how they'd been before.

Think About It

- Do you know anyone serving in the military? Have you ever considered joining the military yourself?

- How would you feel if your parent had to leave home for months at a time?

- How do you think Malik's father feels about his repeated deployments to Afghanistan?

- Have you ever seen someone again after a long absence and thought he or she seemed different?

One spring, Malik's father had been home for almost a year when he announced at the dinner table in a quiet voice, "I've gotta leave again next month."

Malik couldn't believe it. It felt like his dad had barely been home at all. Malik's older sister, Katie, had tears in her eyes. "How long?" she asked in a quivering voice.

> Malik couldn't believe it. It felt like his dad had barely been home at all.

"Twelve months," he said. Katie jumped up from her seat and went running to her room in tears.

"Katie!" Malik's mother yelled after her.

Malik stared at his plate of mashed potatoes and meat loaf. His dad was going to miss the track season again.

Think About It

- why does Malik feel upset that his dad cannot attend his track meets?

- Is there someone in your life who has to leave for long periods of time? How do you feel about it?

Malik tried to spend as much time as possible with his father before he left. His dad helped him

train for the upcoming track season. They went running together every morning and did weight training after school. The whole family spent more time together than usual. Still, Malik couldn't forget that soon his father would be gone again.

On the morning of his father's departure, Malik woke up with the all-too-familiar sick feeling in his stomach. Malik's mother poked her head into his room as he was waking up.

"Oh good," she said. "You're up. Will you get your sister up, too?"

Malik just nodded and rolled out of bed. He walked over to Katie's room and knocked on the door.

"Come in," Katie mumbled.

When Malik opened the door, he saw Katie sitting on the edge of her bed. She was crying.

"Mom says we gotta get up," Malik said with a frown.

Katie just sniffled. Malik turned to leave the room, but hesitated. He had to say something.

"It's okay," Malik said. "He'll come back."

Katie shook her head. "I just hate waiting. Don't you? I'm just so worried something will happen to him."

Malik nodded. "Yeah, I hate it, too."

He knew he probably couldn't make Katie feel better, but she didn't need to feel alone. And neither did he.

Think About It

- Why does Malik feel sick before his father leaves?

- Why do you think Malik decided to talk to his sister?

- Have you ever tried to talk to a sibling when they were upset? Did you help them?

Having a parent in the military isn't easy for a family. One key to dealing with deployment is for the family to keep carrying on with life as best they can. Don't avoid little celebrations just because your father or mother is overseas in a dangerous situation. Take trips to the lake or seashore, just as you would if your parent were home. Go to the movies. Plan fun birthday parties.

If, like Malik, your father has been deployed, celebrate Father's Day anyway, almost as you would if Dad were home. Make a card to send to your father, even if he won't receive it until months later. And throw a party for your dad. You can take pictures and send them to him.

If you don't live life fully while a parent is on a military deployment, it just adds to the stress and loneliness. Your parent who is away will also be glad to know you're having a good time. At the same time, don't ignore your feelings or bury them away. Letting your emotions out is a better way of coping than keeping them inside.

Work It Out

1. Try to live your life as normally as you can, almost as if your missing parent were home. Try to include that parent in your life in indirect ways, like sending pictures and letters while he or she is gone.

2. When you are missing your parent, talk to someone who understands. If you have siblings, they are feeling some of the same emotions that you are. You can also find friends whose parents serve in the military.

3. Don't worry if every once in a while you miss your parent and feel sad. It's normal. Just don't let it keep you from living your life. This is how your parent would want it.

The Last Word from Michael

When a parent is serving in the military, it is very natural that you will miss him or her. You should never be ashamed or try to hide the fact that you are sad because of missing someone you love. But remember that your parent is not far away because he or she wants to be away from you, but because he or she is serving his or her country. By continuing to enjoy your life, you honor your parent's commitment to service.

Families can be a mixed blessing. Sometimes you feel like your family can't understand you and other times it seems they are the only ones who "get it." There are times when you can't understand how you are related to these people. But at the same time, your family can provide you with support, comfort, and love. They can be there for you when you need someone and you, in turn, will be there for them.

Your family is forever a part of you. They know you better than anyone else in the world. And while it can be difficult living with your parents' rules, or having to put up with a bothersome sibling, you'll learn how to handle it. And since the time we spend growing up with our families is short, it's important to try to make the best of this time while we can.

As we grow up, families are important to our development. Our parents and our brothers and sisters help us become who we're meant to become. The times we share with our families, even the difficult times, are the times we often look back on most fondly. When you're older, you may even wish you could go back and enjoy that time all over again.

You can do something to connect with your family right now. You can go into the kitchen or living room or wherever your parents and siblings are and enjoy your family's company today. Be sure to tell them that you love them.

A Guy who's Been There,

Michael

Pay It Forward

Remember, a healthful life is about balance. Now that you know how to walk that path, pay it forward to a friend or even yourself! Remember the Work It Out tips throughout this book, and then take these steps to get healthy and get going.

- Don't worry when you come into conflict with your parents. Part of your parents' job is to make rules. Instead of fighting this, learn to look for compromise. It's far easier for you to gain some freedom when you can be open to give-and-take with your parents.

- Learn to communicate. It's natural as you grow older to want to be independent from your family, but don't avoid them altogether. Force yourself to have a conversation with your parents, and with your siblings, at least once a day. This way, they will know you better and learn to trust you.

- If you miss a father or a family member who is away for some reason, such as military service, try not to dwell on his or her absence. While it can be hard to miss someone who is close to you, your father or mother would want you to enjoy your life.

- Every once in a while, you may find yourself facing a problem in your family that's too big to deal with on your own. For instance, you may be having trouble dealing with your parents' divorce. Don't hold your feelings in. Be brave enough to seek out help and advice from someone older—such as a close relative, a teacher, a coach, or a school counselor.

- If your family has trouble with money, and they could use your help, offer to do what you can. Your contribution will actually help your own situation by relieving stress in the family and keeping everyone happier. Just be sure to work it out with your parents so you still have time for yourself.

- Always try to be patient with younger siblings who sometimes annoy you. Remember that such siblings may simply look up to you.

- No matter what troublesome things may happen in your family as you grow up, there is always hope. Whatever you face, you can pledge to make a positive difference in other people's lives.

Additional Resources

Selected Bibliography

Glennon, Will. *200 Ways to Raise a Boy's Emotional Intelligence.* Berkeley, CA: Conari Press, 2000.

Gurian, Michael. *The Good Son: Shaping the Moral Development of Our Boys and Young Men.* New York: Jeremy P. Tarcher/Putnam, 1998.

Gurian, Michael. *The Purpose of Boys.* San Francisco, CA: Jossey-Bass, 2009.

Kalter, Neil. *Growing Up with Divorce: Helping Your Child Avoid Immediate and Later Emotional Problems.* New York: Free Press, 1990.

Shaffer, Susan Morris. *Why Boys Don't Talk—And Why It Matters: A Parent's Guide to Connecting with Your Teen.* New York: McGraw-Hill, 2005.

Further Reading

Bode, Janet, Stan Mack, and Ronnie Kaufman. *For Better, for Worse: A Guide to Surviving Divorce for Preteens and Their Families.* New York: Simon & Schuster, 2001.

Mosatche, Harriet S., and Karen Unger. *Too Old for This, Too Young for That!: Your Survival Guide for Middle-School Years.* Minneapolis, MN: Free Spirit Publishing, 2005.

Zimmerman, Bill. *100 Things Guys Need to Know.* Minneapolis, MN: Free Spirit Publishing, 2005.

Web Sites

To learn more about coping with family dynamics, visit ABDO Publishing Company online at **www.abdopublishing.com**. Web sites about coping with family dynamics are featured on our Book Links page. These links are routinely monitored and updated to provide the most current information available.

For More Information

For more information on this subject, contact or visit the following organizations.

Boys Town
1-800-448-3000
www.boystown.org
Boys Town is a 24-hour national hotline for immediate help on issues you face, such as chemical dependency, depression, emotional and physical abuse, school issues, sexual abuse, and suicide prevention.

Our Military Kids
www.ourmilitarykids.org
Our Military Kids supports the children of deployed and injured military personnel by providing grants for sports, fine arts, and tutoring. It also provides advice for families dealing with these issues.

Glossary

birth parents
The man and the woman who conceived an adopted child.

custody
The legal arrangement to keep and raise a child.

deployment
When troops are sent to a combat area in readiness for possible military action.

divorce
The legal end of a marriage between two people.

economic
Relating to money.

family tree
A diagram that shows a person's family history.

marijuana
An illegal drug that is usually smoked in a cigarette or a pipe.

permissive parents
Parents who believe that openly showing their children love is the ultimate goal of parenting. These parents tend to avoid conflict with their children, allowing them to do whatever they choose without discipline or limits.

psychologist

A specialist who studies the human mind and how it affects behavior.

rivalry

A competition between people.

role model

A person who sets a good example for others.

temperamental

Being excessively sensitive, irritable, or moody.

Index

About the Author

Michael Fallon is a writer and a nonprofit administrator based in Saint Paul, Minnesota. Michael studied art and English at the University of California, Berkeley, in the late 1980s and later received an MFA in book arts from the University of Alabama. He has worked as a teacher for many years, including two years in the Peace Corps in Poland. Since 1998, Michael has written reviews, feature articles, essays, and profiles for publications such as *City Pages*, the *Orange County Weekly*, the *Pittsburgh City Paper*, the *Pioneer Press*, *Public Art Review*, *Art in America*, and *American Craft*. He has received research grants from Carnegie Mellon University and the Jerome Foundation.

Photo Credits

Mustafa Hacalaki/iStockphoto, cover; Rodrigo Oscar de Mattos Eustachio/iStockphoto, cover; Kent Weakley/iStockphoto, 13; Don Wilkie/iStockphoto, 15; James Pauls/iStockphoto, 16; iStockphoto, 23, 26, 44, 90; Andreas Weber/iStockphoto, 25; Bigstock, 31, 64, 88; Florea Marius Catalin/iStockphoto, 33; Elke Dennis/iStockphoto, 35; Ned White/iStockphoto, 41; James Boulette/iStockphoto, 43; Paul Simcock/iStockphoto, 51; Dra Schwartz/iStockphoto, 53; Jakob Leitner/iStockphoto, 54; Kati Neudert/iStockphoto, 61; Vikram Raghuvanshi/iStockphoto, 62; Fotolia, 71; Brian Toro/iStockphoto, 72; Faruk Ulay/iStockphoto, 74; Michael Jung/Shutterstock, 81; Chris Schmidt/iStockphoto, 83; Wollwerth Imagery/Bigstock, 96; Shariff Che'Lah/Fotolia, 98